A National Theatre of Scotland, 14-18 NOW and Perth Theatre
co-production, in association with Red Note Ensemble

THE 306 : DAWN

WRITTEN BY Oliver Emanuel
COMPOSED BY Gareth Williams
DIRECTED BY Laurie Sansom

RED NOTE

Cast

Nathan Armarkwei-Laryea	Sergeant/Firing Squad/ Witness 2/Corporal/ Private Jack Braithwaite
Emily Byrt	Gertrude Farr
Josef Davies	Private Harry Farr
Scott Gilmour	Private Joseph Byers/ Firing Squad
Peter Hannah	Captain/Prosecutor/ Firing Squad/ Private Thomas Highgate
Steffan Lloyd-Evans	Prisoner's Friend/ Firing Squad
Joshua Manning	Recruiting Sergeant/ Colonel/Firing Squad
Joshua Miles	Lance-Sergeant Joseph 'Willie' Stones/Firing Squad
Jimmy Walker	Private (Dick)/Witness 1/ Firing Squad/ Private Billy Nelson

Musicians

Jonathan Gill	Piano/Musical Director
Robert Irvine	Cello (Red Note Ensemble)
Jackie Shave	Violin (Red Note Ensemble)

Creative Team

Oliver Emanuel	Writer
Gareth Williams	Composer
Laurie Sansom	Director
Becky Minto	Set & Costume Designer
Jonathan Gill	Musical Director
Eddie Kay	Movement Director
Simon Wilkinson	Lighting Designer
Richard Price	Sound Designer
Rebecca Hamilton	Assistant Set Designer
Joseph Brown	Trainee Musical Director
Laura Donnelly	Casting Director

Production Team

Gavin Johnston	Production Manager at Perth Theatre
Carrie Hutcheon	Company Stage Manager
Sandra Grieve	Stage Manager (Company Stage Manager at Perth Theatre)
Emma Whoriskey	Deputy Stage Manager
David Young	Assistant Stage Manager
David Graham	Technical Manager
Helena MacVarish	Site Manager
Andrew Ellis	Lighting Programmer
Paul Froy	Lighting Supervisor
Jock Dinsdale	Lighting Technician at Perth Theatre
Ben Ryan	Lighting Technician
Neil Dewar	Sound Supervisor
Emily Bates	Costume Supervisor
Molly MacDonnell Finlayson	Wardrobe Technician
Jane Hamilton	Press and Marketing Consultant

THE COMPANY WOULD LIKE TO THANK

Donald Grant, Robert Macfarlane, Lindi Wright, Scott Bisset, Lenny Whittet, Lauren Roberts, Edinburgh International Festival Technical Department, MAC cosmetics, Scottish Opera, Scottish Drama Training Network, Professor Gerard DeGroot, Barrowland Ballroom, Kayleigh Olsen, Emma Corfeild, Ben Davies-Coleman, David Innes, Lewis Ho, Alexander Rennie, Margaret Macinnes, The Prince's Trust, Perth and Kinross Council and Perth College.

SPECIAL THANKS TO

Alistair and Pauline Alston

CAST

NATHAN ARMARKWEI-LARYEA

Nathan trained at the Royal Central School of Speech and Drama.

His theatre work includes *Whistle Down The Wind* (Aldwych), *The Lion King* (Lyceum, London), *The Dreaming* (Royal Opera House), *Romeo and Juliet* (Custom Practice/ Exeter Northcott) and *Vernon God Little* (The Space).

His television work includes *Casualty* and *Panorama*. Film work includes *A Long Way Down*.

EMILY BYRT

Emily trained at the Royal Conservatoire of Scotland.

Her previous theatre work includes *Wuthering Heights* (Actors Church, London), *Miracle on 34th Street* (Madinat Theatre, Dubai), *A Matter of Life and Death* (Citizens, Glasgow), *Forest Boy* (St James Theatre, London), *The BFG* (The Lyceum Edinburgh), *Carousel* (New Athenaeum Theatre) and *Spring Awakening* (Cottiers, Glasgow).

Emily was a vocalist on the Susan Boyle concert tour and part of the choreography team for the 2014 Commonwealth Games Closing Ceremony.

JOSEF DAVIES

Josef trained at the London Academy of Music and Dramatic Art.

His previous theatre work includes *Hangmen* (Royal Court, London and London's West End).

His work while training includes *Uncle Vanya*, *The Changeling*, *The Bacchae* and *The English Game.*

Josef's film credits include *The Limehouse Golem*.

SCOTT GILMOUR

Scott trained at the Royal Conservatoire of Scotland. He is an actor and writer.

His previous work with the National Theatre of Scotland includes *Little Johnny's Big Gay Wedding* (with Random Accomplice). Other theatre work as a performer includes *Pressure* (The Lyceum Edinburgh/Chichester Festival Theatre), *James and the Giant Peach* (Dundee Rep), *A Christmas Carol* (The Lyceum Edinburgh), *Everyman*, *Adam & Eve: The Musical* (Splendid Productions), *A Bottle of Wine and Patsy Cline* (Òran Mór) and *The Improvised Musical* (Red Note Ensemble/No Shoes Theatre).

His television work includes *Scrotal Recall.*

Scott is also one half of award-winning music theatre company Noisemaker with composer Claire McKenzie. He has written plays and lyrics for Dundee Rep, The Lyceum Edinburgh, The Arches, St James, London and The Roundhouse. Currently, Noisemaker are working on a new project for the New York Music Festival in July 2016.

PETER HANNAH

Peter trained at RADA.

His stage credits include *Four Play* (Theatre 503), *Shakespeare In Love* (Sonia Friedman Productions), *One Arm* (Southwark Playhouse), *Mock Tudor* (Pleasance Courtyard) and *A Clockwork Orange* (Nottingham Playhouse).

Film and television credits include *Mr Turner* and *Doctor Who.*

STEFFAN LLOYD-EVANS

Steffan trained at the Royal Central School of Speech and Drama.

His theatre work includes *Only The Brave* (Wales Millennium Centre), *Beyond the Fence* (Arts Theatre), *Jack and the Beanstalk* (Yvonne Arnaud Theatre), *The World Goes Round* (St. James Theatre, London), *Godspell in Concert* (UK tour), *Robin Hood* (Hall for Cornwall Trust), *Joseph and the Amazing Technicolor Dreamcoat* (UK Tour), *The Twelve Tenors* (European Tour), *Black Snow* (Moscow Art Theatre), *6: A New Musical* (Twenty Something Productions), *HMS Pinafore, Trial by Jury* (Gilbert and Sullivan Opera Company) and *Tales from the Bad Years* (Landor Theatre).

His television credits include *Pobol y Cwm.*

JOSHUA MANNING

Joshua trained at Bristol Old Vic Theatre School.

His previous theatre work includes *The End of Something* (Old Vic), *The BFG* (Birmingham Rep), *Merlin* (Nuffield), *As You Like It* (Stafford Festival Shakespeare), *Sweeney Todd* (Royal Exchange/West Yorkshire Playhouse), *I Didn't Always Live Here* (Finborough Theatre), *The Magistrate* (National Theatre of Great Britain), *The Deep* (Tobacco Factory, Bristol), *Orphans* (Trafalgar Studios), *King Lear* (Rose Theatre), *The Provoked Wife* (Greenwich Playhouse), *Twelfth Night* (Drayton Arms Theatre), *Bash* (The Lansdown, Bristol), *Fleeing The Nest/Coming to Terms* (Hightide Festival).

His television work includes *Doctors* and *Intergalactic Kitchen.* Film work includes *Muppets Most Wanted* and *Brief Intermission.*

His radio work includes *Romeo and Juliet* and other work for BBC Radio 4 including extracts for BBC Natural Histories.

JOSHUA MILES

Joshua trained at the Guildhall School of Music and Drama.

His theatre work includes *Fuse*, *Romeo and Juliet*, *The History Boys* (Sheffield Theatres), *The Sisterhood* (Belgrade Coventry), *Primetime* (Royal Court, London), *How I Learned To Drive* (Southwark Playhouse), *Stink Foot* (The Yard), *Unidentified Item In The Bagging Area* (Old Red Lion), *All The Ways To Say Goodbye* (Young Vic), *Hansel and Gretel* (Dukes Lancaster), *Pages From My Songbook* (Manchester Royal Exchange), *The Way Of The World* (Chichester Festival Theatre) and *Bully Boy* (St James London/Royal and Derngate, Northampton/Nuffield, Southampton).

His television credits include *Jigsaw*, *Vicious*, *Preston Passion*, *Doctors*, *Holby City*, *The Royal* and *Waterloo Road*.

JIMMY WALKER

Jimmy trained at East 15 Acting School.

His theatre work includes *League of St George* (Pleasance Theatre).

His television work includes *Endeavour* and *Call the Midwife.*

MUSICIANS

JONATHAN GILL

Musical Director/Piano

Jonathan studied with William Mathias at the University College of North Wales and with James Lockhart at the Royal College of Music.

His recent work as a Musical Director includes *The Lion King* (UK tour/Musical Theater, Basel), *The Sound of Music* (Amman Festival, Jordan/Cairo, Egypt), *Oliver* (Sheffield Crucible), *Legacy Falls* (Pearl Theatre, New York), *Gone Fishing* (Linbury Studio, Royal Opera House) and he was Music Director/Arranger for *Charlotte's Web* (Derby Theatre). He was Musical Director on *The Go-Between* (West Yorkshire Playhouse/Derby/Northampton) which won the UK Theatre Award for Best Musical Production 2012 and also on *Follies* (Northampton) and *The Wizard of Oz* (Royal Festival Hall). Jonathan conducted 600 performances of *The Sound of Music* on its UK and Irish tour, starring Connie Fisher.

Jonathan has given premieres of pieces by Jonathan Dove, Richard Taylor, Phillip Cassian, Ian McQueen and Matthew King's *On London Fields* (Royal Philharmonic Society Music Award 2005) and *Odyssean Variations* with cellist Natalie Clein (St Luke's).

ROBERT IRVINE

Cello (Red Note Ensemble)

Robert studied with some of the finest cellists in the world and has held principal positions in the Philharmonia, Scottish Opera and the Academy of St Martin in the Fields. He was a founding member of the Brindisi Quartet, the Chamber Group of Scotland, the Da Vinci Trio and is currently Artistic Co-Director of Red Note Ensemble.

Robert has recorded extensively including *Complete Cello Works of Sally Beamish*, *Cello Works of Giles Swayne*, *'Tree o' licht' Solo Cello Works by William Sweeney*, *Rachmaninov/Shostakovich: Sonatas For Cello And Piano* with Graeme McNaught on piano, *The Cellist of Sarajevo* by David Wilde. His new album *Songs and Lullabies* will be released in September and features 19 new solo cello works and all proceeds will go to UNICEF.

Robert is a Senior Professor at the Royal Conservatoire of Scotland. He plays on a fine cello, a copy of a 1695 Rugeri made in 2014 by Melvyn Goldsmith and a fine bow by the Scottish maker Howard Green.

JACKIE SHAVE

Violin (Red Note Ensemble)

Jackie trained at the Royal Academy of Music and the Britten-Pears School in Snape.

On leaving the Academy she became Leader of English Touring Opera, but soon made the decision to dedicate herself to chamber music, leading the Schubert Ensemble and then co-founding and leading the Brindisi Quartet for fifteen years.

She has appeared as guest leader with many groups including the Nash Ensemble, London Sinfonietta, Composers' Ensemble, Scottish Chamber Orchestra, BBC Scottish Symphony Orchestra and Royal Philharmonic Orchestra. She was appointed leader of Britten Sinfonia in 2005 and in 2013 she became leader of the Red Note Ensemble.

She has also recorded music in other styles including *Postcards from Home,* a world/jazz album in collaboration with Kuljit Bhamra (tabla) and John Parricelli (guitar). She has presented a complete Beethoven string quartet cycle on the Hebridean island of Harris, and gave a free improvisation concert in a cave on Hestur, in the North Atlantic Faroe Islands.

Jackie plays on a Nicola Amati violin, from 1672.

CREATIVE TEAM
OLIVER EMANUEL

Writer

Oliver is an internationally award-winning playwright based in Glasgow.

His previous work for the National Theatre of Scotland includes *Dragon* (with Vox Motus and Tianjin People's Arts Theatre) and *The Day I Swapped My Dad for Two Goldfish*. *Dragon* won Best Show for Children and Young People at the UK Theatre Awards 2014 and was the first play for young people to be performed at the Edinburgh International Festival in 2015. His English version of *Titus* won the People's Choice Victor Award at IPAY 2015. He is a lead writer on *Emile Zola: Blood, Sex & Money* starring Glenda Jackson for BBC Radio 4. Other recent work includes *Prom* (Òran Mór/Traverse/Lemon Tree), *A History of Paper* (BBC Radio 4) and *The Lost Things* (Tortoise in a Nutshell). Oliver was writer in residence for BBC Radio 4 in 2010 and is a part-time Lecturer in Creative Writing at the University of St Andrews.

GARETH WILLIAMS

Composer

Gareth is a Chancellor's Fellow at Edinburgh College of Art. His work seeks to find new participants, collaborators and audiences for new opera and music theatre.

In 2015 he created *Fields of Light* for the BBC Scottish Symphony Orchestra, commissioned by BBC Radio 3, *Let The Dancing Out* for the Maxwell Quartet and he composed, and conducted the premiere of *Hirda*, a new opera he created for NOISE, in collaboration with Shetland fiddler Christopher Stout.

Gareth was Composer in Residence at Scottish Opera from 2011 to 2014. His work there includes *Elephant Angel* (with libretto by Bernard McLaverty) which toured Scotland and Northern Ireland in 2012 and *Last One Out* (with libretto by Johnny McKnight) which premiered at the Sound Festival in 2012 in Fraserburgh Lighthouse. His project *Breath Cycle,* with Gartnavel Royal Hospital, supported by the Wellcome Trust, where he wrote songs and opera specifically for patients with Cystic Fibrosis was shortlisted for a Royal Philharmonic Society Award.

In May 2016, *Rocking Horse Winner,* a chamber opera (with libretto by Anna Chatterton), will be premiered by Tapestry New Opera in Toronto.

LAURIE SANSOM

Director

Laurie is the Artistic Director and Chief Executive of the National Theatre of Scotland. He joined the Company in 2013 and as well as directing *The James Plays* trilogy, which has now played across the world, he directed and adapted *The Driver's Seat* by Muriel Spark in 2015.

From 2006 he was Artistic Director of Royal and Derngate, Northampton, and Associate Director to Alan Ayckbourn at the Stephen Joseph Theatre, Scarborough from 2002 to 2006, where he directed over 20 plays. He was an Arts Council England Trainee Director at the Palace Theatre, Watford, from 1996 to 1997.

He was a member of the National Youth Theatre and the National Student Drama Festival, for whom he has also worked extensively. His productions at Royal and Derngate include; the UK premiere of *Spring Storm* by Tennessee Williams and *Beyond the Horizon* by Eugene O'Neill, which were presented at the National Theatre of Great Britain and led to a nomination for Best Director at the Evening Standard Awards and won him the TMA award for Best Director, and *The Bacchae, Blood Wedding* and *Hedda Gabler*, which were presented as The Festival of Chaos as part of London 2012 Festival.

BECKY MINTO

Set and Costume Designer

Becky has designed a wide range of productions for main-house and touring productions, aerial and dance performances, and site-specific and large scale outdoor events. Her previous designs for the National Theatre of Scotland include *Granite, Truant, A Sheep Called Skye, Transform Fife, The Emperor's New Kilt, The Recovery Position* and *Ignition*, which, along with her design for the site-specific production *White Gold* (Iron-Oxide) was chosen for the exhibition *Make Believe / UK Design for Performance* at the Prague Quadrennial 2015 and the V&A Museum, London. Other theatre work includes designs for The Lyceum Edinburgh, Grid Iron, Visible Fictions, Vanishing Point, Dundee Rep, Fire Exit, 7:84, Walk the Plank, Upswing, Scottish Dance and Citizens Theatre.

Becky was Associate Designer for the Opening and Closing Ceremonies of the Glasgow 2014 Commonwealth Games. Other work in 2016 includes *Hard Times* and *Para Handy* for Pitlochry Festival Theatre.

EDDIE KAY

Movement Director

As a Movement Director, Eddie's previous work with the National Theatre of Scotland includes *Smiler/Hunter*. Other theatre and dance Movement Direction work includes *The Pass*, *You For Me For You* (Royal Court, London), *Brave New World* (Touring Consortium/Royal and Derngate), *Scuttlers* (Manchester Royal Exchange), *The Radicalisation of Bradley Manning*, *Dead Born Grow* (National Theatre Wales), T*he Blue Boy*, *Have I No Mouth*, *This Beach* (Brokentalkers), *Othello* (Frantic Assembly), *Kite* (The Wrong Crowd) and *Bromance* (Barely Methodical Troupe).

As an Associate Movement Director his work includes *Once* (London's West End) and *The Believers* (Frantic Assembly).

As a performer, Eddie's dance, theatre and opera work includes *Beautiful Burnout* (with National Theatre of Scotland), *Hymns*, *Dirty Wonderland*, *Othello* (Frantic Assembly), *Knots* (CoisCéim), *Bird With Boy*, *Five Ways To Drown*, *The Falling Song* (junk ensemble), *The Blue Boy*, *Track* (Brokentalkers) and *Dr Dee* (Rufus Norris and Damon Albarn).

His film work as a performer includes *Cost of Living*, *Round 10* and *Motion Sickness*.

SIMON WILKINSON

Lighting Designer

Simon's previous work for the National Theatre of Scotland includes *Dragon* (with Vox Motus and Tianjin People's Art Theatre), *The Day I Swapped My Dad for Two Goldfish*, *Roman Bridge*, *Truant* and *A Sheep Called Skye*.

Other recent theatre work includes *The Iliad*, *The Weir*, *The Lion, The Witch and The Wardrobe*, *Hedda Gabler*, *The Caucasian Chalk Circle*, *The BFG*, *Bondagers*, *A Christmas Carol*, *Cinderella* (The Lyceum Edinburgh), *The Infamous Brothers Davenport*, *The Not-So-Fatal Death of Grandpa Fredo*, *Bright Black*, *Slick* (Vox Motus), *Grounded* (Firebrand), *Tracks of the Winter Bear* (Traverse), *Light Boxes* (Grid Iron), *After the End*, *Topdog/Underdog* (Citizens, Glasgow), *This Wide Night* (Tron, Glasgow), *Kora* (Dundee Rep), *The Lost Things*, *Feral* (Tortoise in a Nutshell), *Thingummy Bob*, *13 Sunken Years*, *Antigone* (Lung Ha), *Sex and God*, *Pass the Spoon*, *Wild Life* and *After Mary Rose* (Magnetic North).

In 2015 he won the CATS award for Best Design for *Bondagers* (having been nominated in 2009, 2012 and 2014).

RICHARD PRICE

Sound Designer

Richard is currently the Interim Head of Sound at the National Theatre of Scotland. He has previously been Head of Sound at Chichester Festival Theatre, Plymouth Theatre Royal and the Leicester Haymarket. He has also worked extensively with Wildworks Theatre Company and the National Youth Theatre on site specific theatre shows. Richard was Sound Designer for the 2012 Olympic Welcome Ceremonies in the Olympic Village, London and Sound Designer for the Enchanted Palace in Kensington Palace for Wildworks. Other previous sound designs include national tours of *Twelfth Night* and *Measure for Measure*, *The Shape of Things* (London's West End) and various musicals including *Half a Sixpence, Iolanthe, Oklahoma* and *NHS: The Musical* (Theatre Royal Plymouth).

REBECCA HAMILTON

Assistant Set Designer

Rebecca trained at the Royal Scottish Academy of Music and Drama specialising in Set and Costume Design and Scenic Painting. She works as a freelance theatre designer, model maker and scenic artist. She works on a wide diversity of projects from small scale theatre and installation art, to feature films and commercial productions. Rebecca is employed on projects which span theatre, film and television and the visual arts for companies such as National Theatre of Scotland, Vox Motus, Tramway, BBC Scotland, Kelsen and Outland Productions.

NATIONAL THEATRE OF SCOTLAND

The National Theatre of Scotland was established in 2006 and has created over 200 productions. Being a theatre without walls and building-free, the Company presents a wide variety of work that ranges from large-scale productions to projects tailored to the smallest performing spaces. In addition to conventional theatres, the Company has performed in airports, schools, tower blocks, community halls, ferries and forests.

The Company has toured extensively across Scotland, the rest of the UK and worldwide. Notable productions include **Black Watch** by Gregory Burke which won four Laurence Olivier Awards amongst a multitude of awards, the award-winning landmark historical trilogy **The James Plays** by Rona Munro, a radical reimagining of **Macbeth** starring Alan Cumming, presented in Glasgow and at the Lincoln Center Festival and subsequently, Broadway, New York and **Our Ladies of Perpetual Succour**, adapted by Lee Hall from the novel *The Sopranos* by Alan Warner.

The National Theatre of Scotland creates much of its work in partnership with theatre-makers, companies, venues and participants across the globe. From extraordinary projects with schools and communities, to the ground-breaking online **5 Minute Theatre** to immersive pieces such as David Greig's **The Strange Undoing of Prudencia Hart**, the National Theatre of Scotland's aspiration is to tell the stories that need to be told and to take work to wherever audiences are to be found.

Artistic Director and Chief Executive: Laurie Sansom

Chair: Seona Reid DBE

nationaltheatrescotland.com

The National Theatre of Scotland is core funded by the Scottish Government. The National Theatre of Scotland, a company limited by guarantee and registered in Scotland (SC234270), is a registered Scottish charity (SC033377).

14-18-NOW

WW1 CENTENARY ART COMMISSIONS

14-18 NOW is a five-year programme of extraordinary artistic experiences marking the centenary of the First World War. Our programme includes everything from film and music to theatre, fashion and the visual arts, all created especially for 14-18 NOW by leading artists from home and abroad. We're bringing the stories of the war to life, showing how it continues to affect the world in which we live today.

The 306: Dawn is just one of many 14-18 NOW events in Scotland this year. Leith Docks is home to **Dazzle Ship Scotland**, a spectacular new take on wartime 'dazzle' camouflage by Turner Prize-nominated artist Ciara Phillips. The beautiful **Poppies: Weeping Window** sculpture by artist Paul Cummins and designer Tom Piper, already seen by millions around the UK, is currently on display in Orkney and will heading to the Black Watch Museum in Perth at the end of June. Then, in July, the East Neuk Festival stages the world premiere of **Memorial Ground**, a major new choral work by Oscar-nominated composer David Lang in which you can play a part.

14-18 NOW takes place throughout the UK until 2018.

Find out more about all our projects at 1418NOW.org.uk

PERTH THEATRE

Perth Theatre has a long history of artistic innovation and excellence having been at the heart of cultural life in Perth for over a century.

Following a period of restoration and redevelopment, Perth Theatre will reopen in 2017. The £16.6m transformation is a partnership between Horsecross Arts* and Perth & Kinross Council with funding pledges from Perth & Kinross Council, Creative Scotland, The Gannochy Trust, the Heritage Lottery Fund, other trusts and foundations, individual donations and other supporters and funding bodies. The theatre's B listed Edwardian auditorium will be restored to its former glory, a new 200 seat studio theatre will be created along with increased workshop spaces for creative learning and community projects and improved access and audience facilities.

The transformed Perth Theatre will take its place on Scotland's cultural stage as a national inclusive hub with an extensive programme of work including co-production, partnerships, training and community engagement.

While the building is closed Perth Theatre has been going out and about, taking theatre to audiences across the area in pubs, hotels, village halls, community centres and barns!

*Horsecross Arts is the creative organisation set up in 2005 to run Perth Concert Hall and to refresh and reposition Perth Theatre.

www.horsecross.co.uk

Horsecross Arts is funded and supported by:

RED NOTE

Red Note Ensemble is Scotland's contemporary music ensemble, dedicated to developing and performing contemporary music to the highest standards, and taking new music out to audiences around and beyond Scotland.

Red Note is Associate Contemporary Ensemble at the Royal Conservatoire of Scotland in Glasgow, an Associate Company of the Traverse Theatre Edinburgh and Associate Ensemble of the sound Festival Aberdeen. Founded in 2008 by Scottish cellist Robert Irvine, it is directed by John Harris (Chief Executive and Artistic Co-Director) and Robert Irvine (Artistic Co-Director) and led by violinist Jackie Shave. Red Note performs the established classics of contemporary music; commissions new music; develops the work of new and emerging composers from around the world; and finds new spaces and new ways of performing contemporary music to attract new audiences. Red Note's work in 2016 includes a *Reels to Ragas* tour of the Highlands and Islands with Indian tabla player Kuljit Bhamra, a new string quartet for invented instruments by Francois Sarhan, and a largescale co-production and 34 player tour of Europe with Antwerp-based wind ensemble *I Solisti*.

THE 306: DAWN

Oliver Emanuel

THE 306: DAWN

for Caroline,

with love & thanks

OBERON BOOKS
LONDON

WWW.OBERONBOOKS.COM

First published in 2016 by Oberon Books Ltd
521 Caledonian Road, London N7 9RH
Tel: +44 (0) 20 7607 3637 / Fax: +44 (0) 20 7607 3629
e-mail: info@oberonbooks.com
www.oberonbooks.com

A catalogue record for this book is available from the British
Library.

PB ISBN: 9781783197699
E ISBN: 9781783197705

Cover image by Christopher Bowen

Printed, bound and converted
by CPI Group (UK) Ltd, Croydon, CR0 4YY.

for VB

Characters

PRIVATE JOSEPH BYERS OF 1ST ROYAL SCOTS FUSILIERS, from Glasgow, executed aged 17.

PRIVATE HARRY FARR OF 1ST WEST YORKSHIRE, from London, executed aged 25.

GERTRUDE FARR, Harry's wife.

LANCE-SERGEANT JOSEPH 'WILLIE' STONES OF DURHAM LIGHT INFANTRY, from Durham, executed aged 26.

All other parts are played by THE FIRING SQUAD:

RECRUITING SERGEANT

CORPORAL, the jailer.

PRIVATE, from the boat.

CAPTAIN, Harry's CO.

PRISONER'S FRIEND, a Second Lieutenant and defending council.

COLONEL, head of Court-Martial.

PROSECUTOR, a Major.

WITNESSES, another private and a regimental police sergeant.

PRIVATE THOMAS HIGHGATE, the first man to be executed.

PRIVATE BILLY NELSON, executed for desertion.

PRIVATE JACK BRAITHWAITE, executed for mutiny.

SERGEANT, Joseph's NCO.

And other PRIVATES, POLICE and OFFICERS.

A dash (–) indicates an interruption.

An ellipsis (…) indicates a tailing away or a thought-pause.

A line marked … indicates an intention to speak.

Lines marked in bold are sung.

This text went to press before the production opened and so may differ slightly from what was performed.

Acknowledgements

Thank you to Caroline Newall for her support and encouragement of the original idea. Thank you to George Aza-Selinger, Anna Hodgart and everyone at the National Theatre of Scotland.

Thank you to John Harris and the Red Note Ensemble for being with the project from the beginning and trusting us to work with your amazing musicians.

Thank you to my agent Giles Smart and Jennifer Thomas.

Thank you to Lu Kemp and Kirsty Williams for your wise advice on early drafts.

Thank you to all the actors and musicians who developed the play over the last two years and who got the play to where it is.

Thank you to my excellent researcher Sam Tranter.

Thank you to the families Beesleys and Emanuels who put Gareth and I up on our trip to the Somme.

Thank you to our brilliant cast and crew. Thank you to Jonathan Gill, Becky Minto, Simon Wilkinson, and Pamela Walker.

Thank you to Laurie Sansom who believed in the story and the way we wanted to make it.

And thank you to Gareth Williams who came up with this crazy idea in the first place and makes everything sound awesome. Cheers, brother.

1.

HARRY, JOSEPH and WILLIE.

ALL   **I have no name**
no name.

Shot at dawn,
grave unmarked.

I have no name.

Cut me out,
cut me out
like a wart
like an eye.

I have no name.
I have no name.

2.

Early morning. The sun is shining.

HARRY and GERTRUDE lie in bed. They're both in their mid-twenties, working class, from London. They are kissing.

GERTRUDE pushes him away and gets out of bed. She picks up her scattered clothes and dresses.

HARRY whistles.

HARRY	What's your name?
GERTRUDE	Cheeky.
HARRY	Me?
GERTRUDE	You're a bad man, Harry Farr.
HARRY	Guilty as charged.
GERTRUDE	What kind of girl do you think I am? You whistle and I come running.
HARRY	What a world that would be, eh?

GERTRUDE   I'm a respectable married woman, I'll have
            you know. I've got a nice house and a kid.

HARRY   Never! I don't believe it! You're still sixteen
            to me…

GERTRUDE   In your dreams.

HARRY   Come back to bed.

GERTRUDE   I can't spend all day on my back.

HARRY   Why not?

He whistles. She laughs.

HARRY   Don't you remember when you were
            working in the big house in Kensington? I'd
            call round for you on Sundays. That bitch
            mistress never wanted you out of her sight so
            I'd stand round the corner and whistle.

GERTRUDE   She wasn't a bitch. She was looking out for
            me.

HARRY   She thought you were too good for me.

GERTRUDE   And so I was!

HARRY   You're a cruel woman.

GERTRUDE   I could have been a lady's maid by now.
            I could be earning proper money, not
            slumming it with a common soldier.

HARRY   What would you do with money?

GERTRUDE   I know exactly what I'd do.

HARRY   Tell me.

GERTRUDE   I'd buy lots of hats. A hat for every month
            of the year. Every week. Every day. Yes! I'd
            have a different hat for every different day of
            the week and two for church on Sunday. I'd
            have a special room in my house for all the

hats and I'd only wear them once and give them away to the needy.

HARRY   You're cuckoo.

GERTRUDE   Well you married me.

She begins to get dressed.

HARRY   Please don't go. Come back to bed...

GERTRUDE   I've got things to do.

HARRY   No you don't.

GERTRUDE   Are you leaving tomorrow?

HARRY   You know I am.

GERTRUDE   Well then I've got a hundred things to do before then.

HARRY   Not yet, Gertrude, please.

GERTRUDE   There's your uniform to mend, your boots to clean. The kid needs sorting and the house is a mess. I've got to fetch us some dinner for your last meal –

HARRY   Forget about that. I don't care about any of it. I want you –

He makes a grab for her. She skips out of the way.

GERTRUDE   Looks like it's going to be a beautiful day today. The sun is out. Not a cloud in the sky. It's not what I expected.

HARRY   Really?

GERTRUDE   I expected rain. Rain is more fitting isn't it? The sun feels wrong.

In the distance, a gun booms.

HARRY flinches.

HARRY   No. Shit. No, not now. Please god. Shit.

GERTRUDE is dressed.

GERTRUDE   Right. I have to go.

HARRY   No – Gertrude – wait –

The guns fire.

GERTRUDE   Why don't you get a bit more kip, eh? Might
                  be the last time you see a proper bed for a
                  while. We can go for a walk later.

HARRY   G – G – Gertrude!

He reaches out for her but she's gone.

The door is left ajar.

*The sunlight from outside reveals that HARRY is in a shed with stacks
of hay and straw. It's northern France, 1916.*

The guns fire.

HARRY cries out.

*He lifts his hands to cover his face and it's possible to see that his
wrists are shackled. He rocks back and forth.*

A CORPORAL enters.

CORPORAL   Fucking shut it will you, Farr?

*HARRY tries to control himself. He clamps his hand over his mouth
but a whimper escapes him. The CORPORAL raises his stick and
smacks HARRY across the face.*

CORPORAL   Shut it, I said. Shut the fuck up.

HARRY whimpers. The CORPORAL sniffs.

CORPORAL   Fuck. Have you shat yourself again, Farr?
                  You filthy fucking cunt.

The guns fire.

HARRY screams as he is beaten.

3.

Glasgow. The Recruiting office.

Early morning.

A RECRUITING SERGEANT sits in a chair behind a desk piled high with uniforms. He reads a copy of The Herald.

JOSEPH enters and hesitates. He is 17.

The RECRUITING SERGEANT glances up from his newspaper and nods at JOSEPH.

R SERGEANT   Alright, son?

JOSEPH   Alright.

    JOSEPH waits.

JOSEPH   Aye.

R SERGEANT   Aye?

JOSEPH   No I thought you said something.

R SERGEANT   Not me, son.

    He goes back to reading his newspaper. JOSEPH coughs.

JOSEPH   Excuse me, sir.

R SERGEANT   *Sir?* Who you calling sir? Don't see no sirs in here. *(Nods at his stripes.)*

JOSEPH   Is this where I sign up, Sergeant?

R SERGEANT   Sign up?

JOSEPH   Join up. Aye. I mean, join up. The army and that. Is this where folk join up?

R SERGEANT   You seem a bit confused, son. Do you want to come back and try again? *(He notices something in the paper.)* Hold it. The bastards have raised the price of whisky again. It's not Christian.

A new recruit comes in. The RECRUITING SERGEANT stands, gets him to sign the form, hands him a uniform. He points.

R SERGEANT Go through there. Doctor will check you over.

The RECRUITING SERGEANT sits. A beat.

JOSEPH I'm still here.

R SERGEANT Aye?

JOSEPH I can read, you know. Top of my class in reading and writing. The sign on the door says Recruiting Office. I want to be recruited.

R SERGEANT No you don't, son.

JOSEPH Aye I do.

R SERGEANT No you don't. You can't believe the shite you see in the paper. You think it's all fun and games?

JOSEPH But sir – !

R SERGEANT Oi! What did I tell you?

JOSEPH I really do though.

R SERGEANT How?

JOSEPH How? I – I – I want to fight.

R SERGEANT Why don't you run back to the schoolyard, eh? Or go down Celtic Park.

JOSEPH I want to fight for King George.

R SERGEANT King George is a big boy. He can fight his own battles.

JOSEPH But Germany, the bastard Fritz. Kaiser Bill.

R SERGEANT What do you know about it, eh? You've been reading fairy stories before bed? Shouldn't do that. Give you nightmares.

JOSEPH holds his ground.

The RECRUITING SERGEANT sighs, looks him up and down.

R SERGEANT	What's your name?
JOSEPH	Byers. Joseph. Folk call me Joe.
R SERGEANT	Well, Joe. How old are you?
JOSEPH	19.
R SERGEANT	*(Scoffs.)* Pull the other one.
JOSEPH	I am too.
R SERGEANT	Look, Joe. I make the jokes around here. Bugger off back to your mammy.
JOSEPH	I'm 19. I swear it.
R SERGEANT	Alright then. What year were you born, eh?
JOSEPH	1899. No – no I meant –
R SERGEANT	Ahha!
JOSEPH	1895. I meant to say 1895.
R SERGEANT	Not so good at the mathematics? Better luck next time.
JOSEPH	Please.
R SERGEANT	Forget it.
JOSEPH	You have to let me join up. You have to. All the other lads have done it. I – I can't be the only one left behind. They'll kill me.

Silence.

The RECRUITING SERGEANT nods.

R SERGEANT	Go away, Joe.
JOSEPH	But –
R SERGEANT	Go away and come back tomorrow.
JOSEPH	Tomorrow?

R SERGEANT   Aye. Maybe tomorrow you'll have got your
              story straight and you'll have grown a year
              or two. If you know what I mean.

He winks.

JOSEPH twigs and claps his hands.

JOSEPH   Sir! Aye sir!

R SERGEANT   Don't push it, Joe…

JOSEPH   Sorry, Sergeant.

R SERGEANT   Now piss off before I change my mind.

JOSEPH goes.

4.

The FIRING SQUAD.

FIRING SQUAD **First things first**

              you've got to know the facts,

              set down in the military manual

              and the Soldier's Small Book.

              These are the facts.

              Desertion,

              mutiny,

              quitting post,

              leaving the line,

              striking a superior,

              assisting the enemy,

              insubordination,

              cowardice.

              These are crimes punishable by death.

Repeat after me.

The facts.

Desertion,

mutiny,

quitting post,

leaving the line,

striking a superior,

assisting the enemy,

insubordination,

cowardice

are crimes punishable by death.

These are the facts.

You've got to know the facts.

5.

A barn. France, Christmas Eve 1916.

Midday.

WILLIE is in chains, sitting on the floor. He's 26, from Durham. He plays the harmonica to pass the time.

The PRISONER'S FRIEND (a Second Lieutenant and defending council) enters. He carries papers.

PF   Are you Stones?

WILLIE stops.

WILLIE   Excuse me?

PF   *(Reading)* Says here… Lance-Sergeant Joseph
            William Stones.

WILLIE   Aye that's me.

PF	Oh thank god. It's taken me forever to find you. First they sent me out to a place outside Mametz then to somewhere by Fricourt. Trouble is, one barn in France looks roughly the same as another.
WILLIE	You were looking for me…?
PF	Why they can't put everyone in the same place is beyond me. Apparently every available space between here and Amiens is taken up with reinforcements. I know there's a war on but it does make proper bureaucracy so difficult to follow, don't you find?
WILLIE	Who are you?
PF	I'm your Friend.

WILLIE gives him a look.

WILLIE	I don't think so, pal. Never seen you before in my life.
PF	Your Prisoner's Friend.
WILLIE	How's that?
PF	I'm here to defend you at your Court Martial. Every soldier facing trial has the right to have an officer speaking on their behalf. I've been assigned to you for today.
WILLIE	It's today?
PF	Indeed. It's your right to refuse a Prisoner's Friend. You can defend yourself although I wouldn't advise it. In the heat of things, the complications of a trial, the emotions etcetera, a man is likely to loose his head. If you'll pardon the expression. It's best to have someone who's dispassionately in command of the facts. So… Would you be happy for me to be your Prisoner's Friend, Joseph?

WILLIE	Willie.
PF	Sorry?
WILLIE	My name is Willie. My dad was Joseph. I'm Willie.
PF	Do you want me to represent you, Willie?

Slight pause.

WILLIE	Aye – aye that's fine.
PF	Excellent. Shall we get on? We've a bit of a walk ahead of us, I'm afraid.
WILLIE	Don't you want to talk about what happened?
PF	Not at all. I've been given all your information. And I've done this a few times actually.
WILLIE	I didn't do it.
PF	What?
WILLIE	What they said I did. I'm innocent.
PF	That's not really important. It's about what we can prove.
WILLIE	It's important to me.

A beat.

| PF | Of course. Of course, Willie. Come along now. We don't want to be late. |

6.

The boat to France.

Midday.

It's calm and clear.

JOSEPH is vomiting over the rail.

A PRIVATE stares at him. JOSEPH notices. He smiles and wipes his mouth.

JOSEPH	Hiya. How's it going?
PRIVATE	…
JOSEPH	I'm Joseph.
PRIVATE	Eh?
JOSEPH	Joseph's my name. Joe. I'm Joe.
PRIVATE	So what?

The PRIVATE spits.

JOSEPH	Never been to sea before. Seen it. Not been on it. Does it always move this much?
PRIVATE	This is nothing, mate.
JOSEPH	Isn't it?
PRIVATE	Are you joking? It's as calm as anything.
JOSEPH	It's made me a bit sick.
PRIVATE	Smoke?
JOSEPH	Oh aye. Ta.

JOSEPH takes the cigarette. He puts it in his mouth and waits as the PRIVATE lights his own with a match.

JOSEPH copies the PRIVATE and inhales deeply. He coughs.

JOSEPH	Being a soldier's not all it's cracked up to be, eh? There's a lot more waiting. I was hoping for adventure. A week we've been in Folkestone. A whole week! Folkestone's

	not much of an adventure. I wanted to explore but the Sergeant has his eye on me on account of me getting accidentally drunk on our first night. I don't drink. Did you see Folkestone? I heard there was a good pet shop. I fancy a dog. A soldier needs a dog.
PRIVATE	Talk a lot don't you?
JOSEPH	*(Laughs.)* That's what the Sergeant says. Reckon he doesn't like me much.
PRIVATE	Are you Scottish?
JOSEPH	From Glasgow. Can you tell?
PRIVATE	Just a bit. I can hardly understand a word you're saying.
JOSEPH	*(Points.)* Is that France?

The PRIVATE shrugs and smokes. JOSEPH copies.

JOSEPH	You met a lad called Callum?
PRIVATE	Eh?
JOSEPH	Callum. *Callum.*
PRIVATE	No I never did.
JOSEPH	Sure? Tall and ginger. Looks a bit startled. Callum's my best pal. We were in school together. He was a couple of years older. What about Tommy? Or wee Archie?
PRIVATE	*(Shakes his head.)* I don't know what you're saying, mate…
JOSEPH	My whole school signed up, near enough. Callum was the first. I figured we'd all go out together, that we'd all be in the same boat.
PRIVATE	What? Boat? Yeah this is a boat.
JOSEPH	Do you reckon there's someone I can ask?
PRIVATE	Eh?

JOSEPH   About Callum.

PRIVATE   What?

JOSEPH   *(Articulates.)* IS… THERE… SOMEONE… I… CAN… ASK… ABOUT… MY… FRIEND?

PRIVATE   You don't want to ask too many questions. No fucker knows his arse from his tit around here. It's bloody chaos. Right now, I'm wearing two right boots and these trousers are three sizes too big. Wouldn't be surprised if this boat takes a wrong turn and we end up in Australia.

JOSEPH shakes his head.

JOSEPH   Don't know what you're saying, pal. Sorry. Your accent's a bit thick.

The distant boom of guns. JOSEPH jumps.

JOSEPH   What was that?

Another boom.

PRIVATE   That's the guns.

JOSEPH   Is it? Sounds like thunder. Or a heart. It's like a heartbeat, isn't it?

He listens to the guns.

The PRIVATE finishes his cigarette and turns away.

JOSEPH   Goodbye then. What's your name?

PRIVATE   Eh?

JOSEPH   WHAT'S… YOUR… NAME?

PRIVATE   Dick. My name's Dick.

JOSEPH   Thanks for the smoke, Dick. See you around. Think I'm going to be sick again now.

JOSEPH wretches.

7.

The shed. HARRY is getting dressed. He has a black eye, some bruises on his back and sides, and his hands shake. Afternoon. The guns are silent.

A CAPTAIN knocks on the door before entering.

CAPTAIN   Afternoon, Harry. How are we today?

HARRY is surprised.

HARRY   Hello. Who – who is that?

CAPTAIN   It's me, Harry.

HARRY   Lieutenant?

CAPTAIN   Yes. Well actually… *(Nods to his lapel.)*

HARRY   Oh Captain now, is it?

CAPTAIN   Indeed.

HARRY   C – congratulations, C – captain. You must be pleased.

CAPTAIN   Not as special as all that. There was no-one else really. Mother wrote to say that if I last another year they'll probably make me a General!

HARRY   Sure your mother is very proud. Is she keeping well?

CAPTAIN   Frighteningly well, thank you. She's been knitting. Sent me a pair of socks the size of picnic blankets.

HARRY   Nothing like a good pair of socks, Captain.

CAPTAIN   And these are nothing like a good pair of socks! Ha! Indeed… indeed.

The CAPTAIN sniffs. There's a bad smell. He steps back.

HARRY can't do the buttons on his shirt.

HARRY   Could you help me please, sir?

CAPTAIN	Oh rather.

The CAPTAIN button's HARRY's shirt.

CAPTAIN	So… how are you Harry?
HARRY	Good.
CAPTAIN	Honestly?
HARRY	It's the guns. I – I feel fine when there aren't guns. Almost my old self.
CAPTAIN	We're quite near the line here, you know. Guns are a problem.
HARRY	T – tell me about it.
CAPTAIN	What is it, do you think?
HARRY	Same as when I was sick last year. There's nothing physically wrong with me. Lost a bit of weight but otherwise I'm chipper.
CAPTAIN	I saw the Medical Officer's report.
HARRY	He reckons I'm pulling a fast one.
CAPTAIN	I'm sure he doesn't.
HARRY	Yeah he does. Thinks the stammer and the screaming and all that are for show.
CAPTAIN	No-one thinks that.
HARRY	Shellshock. That's what one of the blokes called it. But the MO don't believe in it. Thinks men who cry because of the guns are faking.
CAPTAIN	I admit the MO is not an imaginative man.
HARRY	Why does it happen to me, eh? I've been a soldier forever. Seen it all. How does it take me but not other blokes?
CAPTAIN	I wish I knew, Harry.

HARRY	I can see them looking at me. See them thinking things.
CAPTAIN	What happened to your eye?
HARRY	*(Touches the bruise).* Nothing. I – I fell over.
CAPTAIN	Are you still having nightmares?
HARRY	Yeah.
CAPTAIN	In the day too?
HARRY	Sometimes.
CAPTAIN	Is it always the same?

HARRY nods.

CAPTAIN	Me too.
HARRY	Sir?
CAPTAIN	Never know when they're going to come, do you? I can be out on patrol or simply having my dinner in the mess. I feel quite well. And then I see their faces.
HARRY	Faces?
CAPTAIN	The faces of the men. It's that morning again. 18th September. I'll never forget it. We're about to go over the top. A minute to go. The bombardment is fierce. I'm going up and down the line, chivvying the men. I reach inside my jacket and I – I – I can't find my whistle. I can't find it anywhere. I search my pockets but my whistle isn't there and the attack has begun and the men have gone forward and the machine guns have opened up and I can't find my whistle and the bodies are falling and there's iron in my mouth and I know I could stop it if I could find the blasted whistle but I – I can't.

And I wake up. |

And my dinner is cold and – and – and I can see their faces.

HARRY twitches slightly as the CAPTAIN finishes his story.

CAPTAIN   Do you see them too, Harry?

HARRY nods again.

CAPTAIN   Wish I could get them out of my head. Haven't slept for a month.

The CAPTAIN sniffs again.

CAPTAIN   What's that god awful smell?

HARRY   The river. The Somme. It runs close by the back of this shed.

CAPTAIN   Stinks like a blocked drain, doesn't it?

Silence.

HARRY   Is there any news, sir?

CAPTAIN   Nothing yet, I'm afraid. That's what I came to tell you. The order is yet to be confirmed by the Commander-in-Chief. I made my recommendation for mercy. As did the CO. All we can do is pray that the C-in-C takes your good record into account and sees sense.

HARRY   Yeah.

CAPTAIN   Chin up, Harry. You know what Mother always says.

HARRY   There's nothing to worry about 'til there's something to worry about.

CAPTAIN   Exactly so. Mother is always right.

HARRY   I – I just want to go home.

Slight pause.

CAPTAIN   Is there anything I can do for you, Harry?

HARRY   Not now, Captain. Thank you.

CAPTAIN   If you're sure.

HARRY   Oh actually there is one thing.

CAPTAIN   Name it.

HARRY   Could do with some paper. I've run out. And
                 an envelope if you could spare it. I want to
                 write to my wife.

*The CAPTAIN fishes in his pocket, pulls out a couple of pieces of paper
and an envelope. Also a pencil. He hands them to HARRY.*

CAPTAIN   Here you are.

HARRY holds up the envelope to his chest.

HARRY   **I hear they put it over your heart,**
                 an envelope,
                 over your heart,
                 just here,
                 so the firing squad
                 know where to aim.
                 Just here,
                 over your heart.
                 An envelope,
                 over your heart.

The CAPTAIN pats HARRY on the shoulder.

CAPTAIN   I'll return when there's news. Good man,
                 Harry. Good man.

The CAPTAIN sniffs and exits.

HARRY holds the envelope.

8.

THE FIRING SQUAD choose their rifles.

FIRING SQUAD   **There's a rifle each**
                 each one is loaded

except one
just one
so you'll never know
who fired the fatal shot,
so you'll never have to lie
when you're back home,
you'll never have to say that it was you.

There's a rifle each.

Take one.

They take their rifles, one by one.

9.

A field. Afternoon. It's snowing.

WILLIE is standing in chains, with the PRISONER's FRIEND.

WILLIE	What are we doing here?
PF	This is it.
WILLIE	Eh?
PF	The court. This is where the court is.
WILLIE	It's a field.
PF	It was going to be in HQ but there was a problem with HQ. Last night Fritz scored a direct hit. So now the court will be here.
WILLIE	In a fucking field?
PF	*(Wincing at the expletive.)* Yes it's the best they could do at short notice, I'm afraid.
WILLIE	I was expecting a proper court. Benches. A judge and wigs and that. A building, at least.
PF	Court Martials are often *ad hoc* and close to the battlefield.

WILLIE	*Ad hoc?* What's that?
PF	It'll be fine, Willie. You shouldn't worry.
WILLIE	It's bloody freezing out here.
PF	Looks like we're going to have a white Christmas, doesn't it? I love the snow. I always say it's not really Christmas unless there's snow on the ground.
WILLIE	Where is everyone?
PF	The officers of the court have to come from different regiments. Can't be tried by anyone who knows the accused. It's a devil of a time trying to bring it all together.
WILLIE	Why don't they save themselves the bother and let me get back to my men?
PF	Not long to wait now, Willie. Here we go.

A COLONEL enters with many papers along with two soldiers who carry a table between them. The COLONEL directs them to assemble the court. A couple of chairs, the military code, a gavel, etc.

WILLIE	Who's that?
PF	That's the Colonel from the Royal Kents. He'll be the judge this afternoon.
WILLIE	And the jury? Where's the jury going to be?
PF	No jury.
WILLIE	What? No one else?

The COLONEL sits as several other soldiers in chains parade past the field and exit.

WILLIE	Who are this lot? Do I know them? What have they got to do with my case?
PF	They are the other accused men to be tried.
WILLIE	How many?

PF	Three today, I believe.
WILLIE	*Three?*
PF	It's quite usual. Each case takes no longer than twenty minutes to be heard.
WILLIE	How can he decide whether I'm to live or die in twenty minutes?
PF	There's no time for anything else. There are hundreds of these cases every month, thousands a year.
WILLIE	I – I had no idea…
PF	Well it's not something that the army likes to shout about, to be honest. It's a common offence. But even the condemned are often only sentenced to a loss of rank and put straight back into the line to keep everything ticking along.
WILLIE	Really?
PF	Absolutely. I'm sure that's what will happen to you too.
WILLIE	I told you. I didn't do it.
PF	So there's really nothing to worry about is there?

The PROSECUTOR (a Major) enters and shakes the hand of the COLONEL.

PROSECUTOR	Lovely to see you again, sir. How's your wife?
PF	That's His Majesty's Army.
WILLIE	Who?
PF	He'll be prosecuting on behalf of the army. A barrister in civilian life. A QC.
WILLIE	Do you know him?

PF	He was a couple of years above me at Cambridge.
WILLIE	*(Impressed.)* You were at Cambridge?
PF	I started. Only did a year. Wanted to do my bit so I dropped out.
WILLIE	You're not a proper lawyer then?
PF	Oh no. I read History. Prisoner's Friends don't have to be legally trained. But don't worry. I won't let you down.

The COLONEL takes out a bible. He and the PROSECUTOR place their right hands on it.

WILLIE	What are they doing now?
PF	Taking the oath.
BOTH	I do swear that I will well and truly try the accused person before the court according to the evidence and that I will duly administer justice according to the Army Act now in force, without partiality, favour, or affection. So help me god.

A CORPORAL calls out.

CORPORAL	Court Martial, attention!

Everyone stands to attention.

COLONEL	First case, please.
PROSECUTOR	Lance-Sergeant Stones.

WILLIE steps forward. His chains are removed.

PROSECUTOR	Lance-Sergeant Stones. You're charged with cowardice. The prosecution will seek to show that you did shamefully cast away your arms in the presence of the enemy in the front-line trenches K2 sub-sector on the 26th November, whilst Sergeant of the watch. Do you understand the charge?

WILLIE	Yeah but –
PROSECUTOR	Now to the first –
WILLIE	That's not how it was. Me and the Lieutenant were on patrol and –
COLONEL	Silence.
WILLIE	But you've got it wrong –
COLONEL	We will tell you when you can speak.
PF	Not yet, Willie. Wait.
WILLIE	Oh.
COLONEL	Call the first witness.

The FIRST WITNESS (another Private) steps forward.

PROSECUTOR	Private?
WITNESS 1	Sir.
PROSECUTOR	Tell us what you saw on the night of the 26th November.
WITNESS 1	Just come off guard duty, sir. I was in HQ when Lance-Sergeant Stones appeared. He was shouting about King Crater.
PROSECUTOR	Can you be a little more precise?
WITNESS 1	*(Shouts.)* The Hun are in King Crater! The Hun are in King Crater!
PROSECUTOR	Thank you, Private… Ahem. At what time was this?
WITNESS 1	Just past 2 a.m.
PROSECUTOR	Proceed.
WITNESS 1	We went out. It was bloody murder. *(Coughs.)* Excuse me, sir. It was chaos. The Germans had got into our forward trenches that night and cut off communications. There was a lot of noise and confusion.

PROSECUTOR   Did you speak to the accused?

WITNESS 1   I did. He was Sergeant of the watch. I asked him where his officer was.

PROSECUTOR   Who was his officer?

WITNESS 1   Lieutenant Mundy.

PROSECUTOR   And where was Lieutenant Mundy at this time?

WITNESS 1   Stones said he was wounded.

PROSECUTOR   Did you see the Lieutenant yourself?

WITNESS 1   No, sir.

PROSECUTOR   What did you do next?

WITNESS 1   We went back towards the front line. Down Father's Footpath but not far along, Stones took ill.

PROSECUTOR   How so?

WITNESS 1   He stopped walking. Said his legs had packed in.

PROSECUTOR   Did you assist him?

WITNESS 1   I got him sitting down for a bit. He tried to get up again but he couldn't.

PROSECUTOR   Had he ever complained about his legs before?

WITNESS 1   Not so as I heard.

PROSECUTOR   So he could walk?

WITNESS 1   I don't know. He wasn't wounded or anything. And that's when the Regimental Police Sergeant turned up.

The PROSECUTOR nods. The witness steps down.

COLONEL   Call the next witness.

WILLIE	*(To PRISONER's FRIEND.)* What was that question about? How would that Private know if I'd complained about my legs? He's in another platoon. He doesn't know anything about me.
PF	Now now, Willie.
WILLIE	Is he saying I was feigning?

The SECOND WITNESS (a Regimental Police Sergeant) steps forward.

PROSECUTOR	Regimental Police Sergeant. You were on duty the night of the 26th.
WITNESS 2	Yes, sir. The enemy was attacking our front line trenches. The communications had been cut. I was called in to ensure discipline and forbid retreat.
PROSECUTOR	You're a policeman in civilian life, is that right?
WITNESS 2	Metropolitan Police.
PROSECUTOR	Very good. When did you see the accused?
WITNESS 2	I saw Lance-Sergeant Stones and the private at 2:30 a.m.
PROSECUTOR	Did you speak to him?
WITNESS 2	I asked him what he was doing.
PROSECUTOR	What was his reply?
WITNESS 2	He said he'd been out on patrol with his commanding office Lieutenant Mundy when they'd been set upon by the enemy. Mr Mundy had been shot and told Stones to make a run for it.
PROSECUTOR	Did you see whether the accused had his weapon?
WITNESS 2	He did not.

PROSECUTOR   Definitely?

WITNESS 2   No, sir.

PROSECUTOR   Did you question him about it?

WITNESS 2   I did.

PROSECUTOR   And?

WITNESS 2   He said the enemy chased him down the trench. He dropped his rifle to block the way.

PROSECUTOR   How did your questioning of the accused continue?

WITNESS 2   I ordered him and the Private back to the front line.

PROSECUTOR   What was his response?

WITNESS 2   He asked permission to smoke.

PROSECUTOR   Smoke?

WITNESS 2   Yes, sir.

PROSECUTOR   Did you give it?

WITNESS 2   No. I repeated my order to go back to the front line.

PROSECUTOR   Did he go?

WITNESS 2   No.

PROSECUTOR   What was his condition?

WITNESS 2   He seemed exhausted. He was trembling.

PROSECUTOR   Trembling?

WITNESS 2   Like he was afraid.

COLONEL   Define afraid, please.

WITNESS 2   He seemed thoroughly done up.

WILLIE   *(To PRISONER'S FRIEND.)* How can he know? I was unwell. I couldn't move.

PROSECUTOR	And then what happened?
WITNESS 2	I arrested Lance-Sergeant Stones, charging him with casting away his arms.

The PROSECUTOR nods. The SECOND WITNESS steps down.

COLONEL	Do we have the medical report on Lance-Sergeant Stones?
PROSECUTOR	Here, sir. *(He holds up a file.)*
COLONEL	What are its findings?
PROSECUTOR	Upon examination the Medical Officer found nothing physically wrong with the accused.
COLONEL	Had he ever reported sick before?
PROSECUTOR	On two previous occasions.
COLONEL	For what reasons?
PROSECUTOR	It says here…for rheumatic pains in his legs.
WILLIE	*(To PRISONER'S FRIEND.)* I told you I wasn't faking.
COLONEL	Call Lance-Sergeant Stones.
PF	It's you now, Willie.
WILLIE	What should I say?
PF	The truth. Just tell the truth.

WILLIE steps forward.

COLONEL	Tell us what happened, Lance-Sergeant.
WILLIE	Lieutenant Mundy and myself were out on patrol. The enemy was all over us. Raids all along the front line. The night was wild. Lots of gunfire and shouting. Me and the Lieutenant had come into King Crater where there was a flash. The Lieutenant fell. He cried out. My god, I'm shot! It was all across

his chest and legs. Blood. He pushed me away and said: For god's sake Sergeant go for help, go, go! Fritz was racing towards us. I stuck my rifle across the way and ran.

PROSECUTOR   How many of the enemy did you see?

WILLIE   Four or five. I don't know the precise number. It happened very fast.

PROSECUTOR   Was your rifle loaded when you dropped it?

WILLIE   I didn't drop it. I put it across the trench.

PROSECUTOR   Was it loaded, Lance-Sergeant?

WILLIE   Yes.

PROSECUTOR   So why didn't you fire?

WILLIE grins.

PROSECUTOR   Did I say something funny?

WILLIE   Not at all, sir. I was wondering… have you ever fired a rifle yourself?

PROSECUTOR straightens.

PF   *(Whispers.)* Answer the question, Willie.

WILLIE   My rifle was loaded –

PROSECUTOR   Ah.

WILLIE   But the safety was on and the cover was over the breach. It would've taken too long to return fire.

PROSECUTOR   Why didn't you remove the cover?

WILLIE   I had orders.

PROSECUTOR   From whom?

WILLIE   My commanding officer.

PROSECUTOR	Why would Lieutenant Mundy issue the orders to keep your rifle covered if there were German raids?
WILLIE	We didn't know we were hot.
PROSECUTOR	Hot?
WILLIE	We didn't know that Fritz was in our area. Not at first. It was a normal patrol. It was muddy. I needed to keep my rifle clean.
PROSECUTOR	Unfortunately the Lieutenant did not survive to verify your story –
WILLIE	It's not a story. It's what happened.
PROSECUTOR	Do you think your actions constitute fit behaviour for a man of your rank?
WILLIE	What else could I have done?
PROSECUTOR	You could've fought the enemy. You could have stayed with your fallen officer.
WILLIE	My duty was to do as I was ordered and report the attack to HQ.
PROSECUTOR	You weren't motivated by fear?
WILLIE	How do you mean?
PROSECUTOR	You are on a regular patrol, unaware of any immediate danger when your officer is shot and the enemy is charging towards you. Fear is what any man would feel.
WILLIE	I wasn't afraid.
PROSECUTOR	No?
WILLIE	No. I blocked the way. And it worked didn't it? No one's complaining Fritz made it through are they?

PROSECUTOR	Why didn't you return to the line once you had told HQ about Lieutenant Mundy's wound?
WILLIE	I had trouble with my legs.
PROSECUTOR	Can you explain this trouble?
WILLIE	Not clearly… no.
PROSECUTOR	You'll have to do a little better than that, Lance-Sergeant.
WILLIE	They stopped working. I'd trouble with them before. Pain. I – I couldn't move them. Couldn't take a step… I don't know… I don't know how to explain it.
PROSECUTOR	That's all I have to ask at this time.
COLONEL	Is there anything else that the accused or his Prisoner's Friend wishes to say at this time?

The PRISONER'S FRIEND steps forward.

PF	Yes, sir.
COLONEL	Go on.
PF	It's worth repeating that at no point did Lance-Sergeant Stones hide. He did as he was ordered by his commanding officer and reported to HQ. HQ knew of his whereabouts at all times. Furthermore I put it to the Court Martial that there is no clear proof of cowardice against Lance-Sergeant Stones but rather he acted bravely in stopping the enemy breach further into our trenches.
COLONEL	Very well. We will consider our verdict.

The COLONEL makes notes and flicks through his papers.

WILLIE	What was all that stuff about the breach? Fitting behaviour for a man of my rank…?

PF	They have to ask the question.
WILLIE	They're making me out to be someone I'm not. I'm a coward and there's nothing else to it.
PF	I'm it will be fine. It's procedure, that's all.

10.

The same.

One by one, the accused men step forward in chains and make their case.

COLONEL	Private Thomas Highgate. You are charged when on active service of deserting His Majesty's Service.
THOMAS	**I – I don't remember exactly what happened. I got strolling about, went down to a farm, lay down –**
COLONEL	Private Billy Nelson. You are charged with repeated acts of desertion.
BILLY	**I've had trouble at home. My mother died, leaving my sister aged 13, my brother aged 10. I am the only one left. I'd no intention of deserting.**
COLONEL	Private Jack Braithwaite. You are charged with mutiny against officers of His Majesty's Service.
JACK	**I'm not a soldier, erm... I'm a bohemian journalist. I came for glory and honour and glory. Instead I've won only shame, disgrace.**
ALL	**Only shame, disgrace... I came for glory and honour and glory. Instead I've won only shame, disgrace...**

The COLONEL slams down his gavel.

COLONEL   **We will consider our verdict.**

11.

The same.

WILLIE shakes his head.

WILLIE   What's happening now?

PF   It's over.

WILLIE   They think I'm guilty already.

PF   I'm sure not. All we can do is wait.

12.

HARRY writes his letter. The shed. Late afternoon.

It's hard work. The guns are firing and HARRY's hand shakes terribly. He gives up. He tries again. He gives up. He tries again.

GERTRUDE enters, watches.

The guns continue.

13.

A trench. Dusk.

There is snow on the ground as JOSEPH and the SERGEANT stand watch. There's a small fire in a brazier at their feet.

JOSEPH   It's Baltic out here. How is it so cold?

SERGEANT   Shut up, will you?

JOSEPH   This is worse than Glasgow. Why couldn't
            we have gone to Africa or somewhere?
            Africa would be lovely and warm. I need
            another pair of socks. I've run out. If I had
            another pair of socks I could cover my

hands. Look. My breath's coming out in smoke.

SERGEANT shakes his head.

SERGEANT You don't know what shut up means, do you Byers?

JOSEPH Sorry, Sergeant.

SERGEANT We've only been on duty an hour. There's another five to go. Talking about the cold won't make it go away.

JOSEPH If I don't talk I'll freeze to death.

SERGEANT Suits me. At least if you did, I could get some peace and quiet.

A shell falls very close.

JOSEPH Bloody hell! Was that for us?

SERGEANT Misfire, I reckon.

JOSEPH Ours or Fritz?

SERGEANT Fritz. They're trying to break up the line as we retreat.

JOSEPH Can't they leave us alone for a day? Just a day? Or a week even? If everyone stopped fighting for a week then we could go and warm up a bit.

SERGEANT I can't tell sometimes whether you're an anarchist or a fucking idiot…

JOSEPH I heard that some of the lads played football with Fritz at Christmas. There was a truce and everyone went into No Man's Land.

SERGEANT Bollocks.

JOSEPH It's what I heard.

SERGEANT Oh forget it. Why don't you keep on talking, Byers? I'm going to close my eyes for ten

minutes. I'm dead on my feet. Kick me if an
officer comes along.

JOSEPH   Yes, Sergeant.

The SERGEANT settles into the corner before promptly falling asleep.
JOSEPH lights his cigarette with a match. The SERGEANT snores.

JOSEPH   **I never liked the dark. I was born in
the city. I like the lights and the shout
and the people. And I couldn't close
the curtains and I couldn't go to sleep.
Thought I'd wake up dead if I slept too
deep. I never liked the dark. I haven't
slept a wink since I arrived. The light
is disappearing and I'm here shivering,
afraid of everything. Even being afraid.
(Laughs.) Ha! And this fire is almost out.
Oh this fire is almost out.**

Fuck. Excuse my French.

**But where is the dawn? Where is the
dawn? When will the sun come out? I
can't stand these endless nights. They feel
like a hand around my throat. A little
light... is that too much to ask? I never
liked the dark. What's wrong with me?
Why can't I be brave like him? Where
is my stiff upper lip? I'm scared of every
sound, everything, all the time! I never
liked the dark. This fire is almost –**

The fire is out.

JOSEPH   Sergeant? Sergeant?

SERGEANT   …

JOSEPH   Fire's gone out.

SERGEANT   …

JOSEPH hesitates and then runs off. The guns fire.

14.

HARRY is continuing to write his letter. GERTRUDE comes closer, looks over his shoulder before snatching the paper away. The guns are not far away.

She reads.

GERTRUDE   What is this? Is this for me?

HARRY   G – Gertrude?

    She holds up the letter, tears in her eyes.

GERTRUDE   What are these words, Harry? What are you trying to say? I'm reading them but I don't understand.

HARRY   Please don't be upset…

GERTRUDE   Says here you spent two months in hospital but no one could work out what was wrong. Why didn't you tell me?

HARRY   There was nothing wrong.

GERTRUDE   Two months!

HARRY   The doctor said I was fine. Wouldn't even give me a stripe.

GERTRUDE   Two months and not a word!

HARRY   I – I wasn't wounded.

GERTRUDE   Oh no? Show me your hand.

HARRY   Eh?

GERTRUDE   You heard.

HARRY   *(Puts his hand in his pocket.)* I'm not a p – p – performing monkey.

GERTRUDE   Can't do it, can you Harry? 'Cos your hands shake like a leaf in a storm.

    He snatches the letter and tears it up.

HARRY	What do you want me to say? I had to go back.
GERTRUDE	Why?
HARRY	It's my duty.
GERTRUDE	Your duty?
HARRY	There's a bloody war on, woman! If I didn't go back then they'd call me a c – coward.
GERTRUDE	You are a coward. Couldn't even tell your wife.
HARRY	D – don't say that.
GERTRUDE	What? It's the truth isn't it?
HARRY	G – G – Gertrude, p – p – please.
GERTRUDE	*(Shakes her head.)* I don't know who you are anymore, Harry. I don't know who this man is. He's not the Harry I know.

The guns fire. Another HARRY enters and begins to twitch.

HARRY	Who are you? Who is he? What's going on?

The other HARRY twitches repeatedly. HARRY tries to keep control of himself but is compelled to mirror the actions.

GERTRUDE	**Who are you, Harry? Where have you gone?**

The guns fire.

Another HARRY enters and another and another and another. Each of them twitches, falls, cries out, jumps.

GERTRUDE	**Where's that brave man I used to love? Where's the man who wouldn't flinch, who wouldn't run?**
HARRY	G – Gertrude. I – I – I –
GERTRUDE	**I don't know this man, this man who shakes and screams. Who is he? I don't**

know this man who is afraid. Who are you, Harry?

HARRY   It's n – n – n – not me –

GERTRUDE   **Who are you? Where have you gone? Where's that brave man I used to love? Where's the man who wouldn't flinch, who wouldn't run? Who are you, Harry? Where have you gone?**

HARRY can't cope. He stumbles.

And then a whistle blows. The walls of the shed collapse. It's 18ᵗʰ September 1916. Machine guns and smoke.

A dead soldier appears and holds out a rifle to HARRY. He shakes his head. He screams. He tries to run to GERTRUDE but she has disappeared.

The dead soldiers climb the trench, everyone except HARRY. HARRY is beside himself, clutches his chest and convulses.

The machine guns fire and the dead soldiers fall back, get up, fall back, get up, fall back, get up. HARRY collapses.

15.

The PRIVATE (from the boat) is playing cards with four other soldiers around a small fire. It's night. Cold. A little way off, an officer plays the cello.

PRIVATE 2   Have you got a heart?

PRIVATE 3   Nope.

PRIVATE 4   No.

PRIVATE 5   Don't look at me.

PRIVATE 2   Come off it. One of you bastards has a heart. I know it.

PRIVATE 3   I might have a heart if you've got the seven of clubs.

PRIVATE 2   Fuck off.

JOSEPH enters.

JOSEPH   Dick? Is that you?

The SOLDIERS watch JOSEPH as he approaches. The PRIVATE says nothing.

JOSEPH   It's me. Joe. From the boat. You remember me, don't you?

PRIVATE 4   Oh Dickie boy…

PRIVATE 5   It's Joe from the boat, Dick!

PRIVATE 2   Dick, your bird's here!

The SOLDIERS laugh. JOSEPH laughs too. The PRIVATE gives them a look.

JOSEPH   I got a bit lost. It's pretty dark, eh?

PRIVATE   What do you want?

JOSEPH   What are you playing?

PRIVATE 3   *(Shrugs.)* Cards.

JOSEPH   Is it fun? Can I play?

PRIVATE   No.

JOSEPH   I promise I won't talk.

PRIVATE   Piss off, will you?

JOSEPH   Don't be like that, Dick. I'm knackered. I've been ducking in and out of ditches all night. There are police everywhere on account of the retreat. I figure they wouldn't be too chuffed with me paying a visit to my best pal Dick. *(He spots the officer playing the cello.)* Oh. Is that officer safe?

PRIVATE 4   He's drunk.

JOSEPH   Drunk?

PRIVATE 4	After what happened this morning. He's been drinking the whole day.
PRIVATE 5	How does he do it?
PRIVATE 2	He bribes the Quarter Master for extra rum ration.
PRIVATE 5	Wanker.
JOSEPH	What happened this morning?
PRIVATE	Nothing. Nothing happened this morning.

Silence.

JOSEPH	Go on. Tell me a story. Everything is so boring.

Slight pause.

PRIVATE 4	Well this morning –
PRIVATE	No.
PRIVATE 5	What's the problem, Dick?
PRIVATE	We said we wouldn't talk of it. We agreed.
PRIVATE 5	Did we?
JOSEPH	What happened?
PRIVATE	Go back to your own platoon, Joe. Before you get us all in the shit.
PRIVATE 5	Why can't the lad know?
PRIVATE 2	He's got to learn hasn't he?
PRIVATE	Not him.
PRIVATE 2	Why not?
JOSEPH	Why not, Dick? I've got to learn.

The PRIVATE shrugs.

JOSEPH	Brilliant.

JOSEPH joins the circle. The PRIVATE moves away, lights a cigarette.

PRIVATE 5	The Sergeant woke us up. 3 a.m. Still dark. We figured Fritz must've broken through the line and we were retreating again. The Sergeant took us to a shed at the edge of the wood. In the shed we were told to choose rifles. There were five of us and five rifles. Sergeant said that four of the rifles were loaded and one of them wasn't –
PRIVATE 2	We would never know who fired a real shot –
PRIVATE 3	But we did know because one of them was lighter than the others. Stands to reason –
PRIVATE 5	Who's telling this story?

The others say nothing.

PRIVATE 5	We had to choose rifles. We went out of the shed and formed a line. We waited about half an hour before an ambulance showed up. The back doors are opened and out comes a bloke from the King's Royal Rifles. We didn't know his name. He was in chains. Blindfolded. The Sergeant tied him to a post, stuck an envelope over his heart like this *(Holds a playing card up to his chest.)* then we – we –
PRIVATE	We shot him. End of story.

JOSEPH shakes his head.

JOSEPH	You killed him?
PRIVATE	Yes.
PRIVATE 2	Not immediately. A couple of blokes missed.
PRIVATE 3	What? Don't look at me.
PRIVATE 2	Did I say anything?
PRIVATE 4	My hand is still shaking. Look. *(Holds out his hand.)*

PRIVATE 2	The first shots didn't kill him. The Captain had to finish him off with his revolver. He's been pissed and playing like that ever since.
JOSEPH	I don't get it. What had he done?
PRIVATE 5	He was a deserter.
PRIVATE 2	It was an open and shut case. He was caught in a village about ten miles from here in his civvies.
PRIVATE 5	I heard it wasn't his first time.
PRIVATE 4	I heard he was Irish.
PRIVATE 5	I heard he had a lass in Amiens.
PRIVATE 3	He was always chasing cunt.
PRIVATE 2	No he was going to marry the girl and get back to Blighty.
PRIVATE 5	What? How would he do that?
JOSEPH	That – that's a terrible story.
PRIVATE	Is it? Why?
JOSEPH	He was one of us.
PRIVATE	No. He walked away. He knew what he was doing and what would happen if he got caught. We're at war. This is the British army. It's not like any other job. We have to stand. It's our duty. If I don't know that the bloke next to me is going to hold his position then how can I fight? He puts everyone at risk. We all want to go home. Shit, I lie in my bunk every night dreaming of sitting in my local, my girl beside me, a pint in my hand. Who doesn't? No one in their right mind wants to be here. Fear is normal. That's why we got to have discipline. And do you want to know the truth…? It doesn't even matter if that fucking bloke was guilty. Maybe he did

it, maybe he didn't. I don't know. The point is that he's an example. To all of us. This is a battlefield and we are fighting an enemy and any measure is necessary to win that fight. At the end of the day, men will die. It's up to you whether you die fighting or get killed by your own side. I know which I'd rather.

Silence.

PRIVATE 4   My hand's still shaking.

PRIVATE 5   He was strong at the end, wasn't he? Didn't cry out. He stood up.

PRIVATE 3   He did. Yes.

The OFFICER continues to play.

PRIVATE   Is he ever going to stop playing that thing? It's doing my fucking head in.

Slight pause.

PRIVATE 2   Are we playing this game or not?

PRIVATE 3   We're playing.

PRIVATE 2   Where were we?

PRIVATE 3   You were going to give me all your money.

PRIVATE 2   Funny boy.

PRIVATE 5   New deal?

PRIVATE 3   Pass me the cards.

PRIVATE 4   My hand's still shaking. I don't understand it.

PRIVATE   Go home now, Joe.

JOSEPH   Got anything to drink, Dick? I'm thirsty.

The PRIVATE holds out his canteen. JOSEPH reaches for it. The PRIVATE holds it back.

PRIVATE   You can have one gulp. Then go.

JOSEPH   Actually I was hoping I could stay with you.
                   Transfer to your regiment. I don't really have
                   any pals and the Sergeant doesn't like me
                   much –

PRIVATE   One gulp. And go.

JOSEPH takes the canteen.

JOSEPH   Was it true? What you said about that bloke.

The PRIVATE nods.

JOSEPH hands back the canteen without drinking.

JOSEPH   On second thoughts, I should go. I – I've got
                   a long walk. See you around, Dick.

JOSEPH goes.

PRIVATE   See you, Joe.

*The PRIVATE watches JOSEPH disappear into the night. The
OFFICER continues to play.*

16.

The moon is shining through a crack in the roof.

GERTRUDE is brushing her hair.

HARRY wakes from his nightmare. He is sweating and distraught.

HARRY   What – what? Who are you?

GERTRUDE   Harry.

HARRY   Gertrude? Is that you?

GERTRUDE   Who else would it be?

HARRY   W – where are the others?

GERTRUDE   Others?

HARRY   ...

GERTRUDE   There's only you and me.

HARRY   Are you sure?

GERTRUDE   Course, Harry. You were asleep.

He shakes his head.

HARRY   I was having a terrible dream. You were
               here but you weren't you, you looked like
               you but... and there were these soldiers and
               they... we were back in the trenches and –

               (Slight pause.) What – what time is it?

GERTRUDE   Late.

HARRY   How late?

GERTRUDE   You've been in bed most of the day.

HARRY   Have I? Shit.

GERTRUDE   Hush now. It's alright. You needed the rest.

HARRY   I feel exhausted.

GERTRUDE   Well shut your eyes for a bit longer then.

HARRY   I couldn't.

GERTRUDE   Tell me more about your dream then. What
               was I doing?

HARRY   I – I don't recall.

GERTRUDE   Go on, Harry. I won't blush.

HARRY   It wasn't like that. I – I don't want to talk
               about it. I want to talk about you. I want to
               be with you, here. Now. It's my last night.

*He gets up, kisses her and takes her hairbrush. He starts brushing
it for her.*

GERTRUDE   **Look, Harry, the moon. How big it is.**

HARRY   **It's a Sniper's Moon, that's what they call
               it. They see us by it's light, pick us off at
               night –**

69

She shakes her fist at the moon.

GERTRUDE   **Horrid, wicked thing. I won't look at it again.**

HARRY   I'm sorry, Gertrude –

GERTRUDE   Why?

HARRY   *(Shakes his head.)* It's just the moon. I don't know why I keep ruining things, I – I should keep my mouth shut.

I – I shouldn't have said anything.

GERTRUDE   **No, Harry. I want you tell me things. I want you to tell me everything, Harry.**

He shakes his head.

HARRY   **There are some things that should never be said. There are some things that should never be said.**

GERTRUDE   **Harry, tell me things.**

HARRY   **There are some things that should never be said. There are some things that should never be said.**

GERTRUDE   **Tell me those things that should never be said.**

HARRY   **There are some things that I want to forget. There are some things that I want to forget.**

GERTRUDE   **I'm your wife, Harry. Tell me those things that you want to forget. Tell me those things that you want to forget.**

HARRY   **I don't have**
I don't have
I don't have words.

GERTRUDE **What's mine is yours,**
          what's yours is mine.

HARRY   **I don't have**
          I don't have
          I don't have words.

          I don't have
          I don't have
          I don't have words.

          I don't have
          I don't have
          I don't have words.

GERTRUDE **Show me where it hurts and I can make**
          it better.

She takes him in her arms.

GERTRUDE I wish I could crack your head open. Like an
          egg. Get inside your brain and see what was
          going on in there.

HARRY   Me too.

17.

The field. It's dark. Snow falls.

WILLIE is shivering, holding his hand to his chest.

PF   Are you alright, Willie?

WILLIE   My chest hurts. Heart's beating like the clappers.

PF   Not long now.

They wait.

18.

The shed. GERTRUDE laughs.

GERTRUDE   **Do you remember when we first met? You couldn't dance a step.**

HARRY   I remember.

GERTRUDE   **Two left feet and pointy elbows.**

HARRY   *(Laughs.)* Ha. I remember.

GERTRUDE   **I taught you how to move, step by step.**

HARRY   I remember.

GERTRUDE   **And now you're the greatest dancer in the world.**

HARRY   Steady…

GERTRUDE   **The greatest dancer in our street.**

HARRY   Possibly.

GERTRUDE   **I taught you to dance, Harry. I'll teach you how to forget…**

She pulls him to her and they dance round and round and round the shed in the light of the moon. It is magical.

19.

JOSEPH is walking along the road. A regimental POLICE OFFICER steps out, holding a lantern.

POLICE 1   Well hello there, Private. Where do you think you're going?

JOSEPH   *(Opens mouth.)*…

POLICE 1   Speak up.

JOSEPH   I – I was fetching coal. Sergeant sent me.

POLICE 1   Is that so? What's your name?

JOSEPH   Byers, Joseph.

POLICE 1   Regiment?

JOSEPH   1st Royal Scots.

POLICE 1   Well that's unfortunate.

JOSEPH   How?

POLICE 1   1st Royal Scots are on the front line. Which is
               ten miles that way. (*He nods over his shoulder*).

JOSEPH runs. The regimental POLICE OFFICER gives chase.

20.

The shed. A knock on the door. The CAPTAIN enters.

HARRY and GERTRUDE stop.

CAPTAIN   E – evening, Harry. At ease.

HARRY   C – c – captain, sir.

GERTRUDE moves into the shadows.

21.

*Another regimental police officer steps out, with another lantern, blocking
the way.*

POLICE 2   Oh no you don't. You'll not get away that
               easy –

*JOSEPH ducks round him and continues to run. The regimental
POLICE OFFICERS give chase.*

JOSEPH trips and falls.

*The regimental POLICE OFFICERS grab him. JOSEPH kicks and
screams.*

JOSEPH   No! Get off me! No! No! No!

22.

The shed.

GERTRUDE smiles and disappears. HARRY reaches out.

HARRY   Don't go, G – G – Gertrude…

She is gone.

23.

The field. WILLIE and the PRISONER'S FRIEND. COLONEL steps forward.

COLONEL   Court Martial, attention!

The Court Martial stands to attention. The COLONEL reads his verdict.

COLONEL   **The finding of this Court Martial is that Lance-Sergeant Stones is guilty –**

WILLIE stumbles.

PF   Willie!

WILLIE straightens. He is able to stand. He is sweating with the effort.

COLONEL   **The finding of this Court Martial is that Lance-Sergeant Stones is guilty of cowardice. The penalty is death. This order to be confirmed by the Commander-in-Chief. Take him away.**

WILLIE   Who is talking about? Is he talking about me? He can't be talking about me because I didn't do it. I told them didn't I? I didn't do it.

24.

The shed. Night.

The CAPTAIN *clears his throat.*

CAPTAIN   I – I – I'm afraid I have bad news, Harry. The Commander-in-Chief has confirmed the order for e – execution.

Silence.

HARRY   When, sir?

CAPTAIN   B – beg pardon?

HARRY   When is it happening?

CAPTAIN   Immediately. That's to say, at dawn.

HARRY   And what time is that?

CAPTAIN   Not long.

HARRY   Thanks for coming to tell me yourself, Captain. I appreciate it.

The other condemned men are in their cells. [The action is simultaneous but each character is in a different place in reality].

SERGEANT   Byers?

JOSEPH   Joe.

SERGEANT   Eh?

JOSEPH   You can call me Joe, Sergeant. I'm Joe.

SERGEANT   What the fuck do I care? You're to be executed in the morning.

PF   How are you, Willie?

WILLIE   I was writing to my sister. Don't know whether the letters get through with the fighting but you can only hope can't you?

CAPTAIN   This. It's not what I wanted. I – I told the CO and he passed it up the chain of

75

command. We know you've fought bravely in the past. You were unwell. You shouldn't have been put back in the line. I – I'm most awfully sorry.

HARRY   Sir.

SERGEANT   Byers? Byers?

CAPTAIN   My recommendations went right to the top. But what with the Big Push and these reinforcements. The C-in-C couldn't let it pass. An example had to be made. A matter of discipline.

It's n – nonsense, of course.

HARRY   Yeah.

SERGEANT   Byers are you hearing what I'm telling you? You're to die. I have the order.

JOSEPH   I – I don't understand.

SERGEANT   You are a fucking idiot, aren't you?

JOSEPH   I plead guilty. They said if I plead guilty that they'd go easy on me.

CAPTAIN   I – I – I wish there was something else I could do.

HARRY   Please don't trouble yourself, Captain.

Harry stops.

HARRY   My stammer. It's gone. Listen. I can say Captain, Captain.

CAPTAIN   J – jolly good!

HARRY and the CAPTAIN smile.

The PRISONER'S FRIEND glances at the CORPORAL at the door. He lifts his shirt.

PF   Willie. I've a revolver here.

WILLIE	Eh?
PF	A revolver.
WILLIE	What on earth – ?
PF	If you'd like it. If you felt you couldn't face –
WILLIE	No!
PF	It's not cowardice to choose your own way out. I know what I'd want.
WILLIE	I'm going see it through.
PF	Why for god's sake?
WILLIE	I'm guilty in the eyes of the law. There's enough shame in that. I'll not disgrace my family any more.
SERGEANT	You're a fucking coward and you're going to die like a fucking coward.
WILLIE	Do you think I'm a coward?
HARRY	Have you any paper, Captain?
WILLIE	*(Shakes his head.)* You don't have to answer that.
JOSEPH	Who'll tell my mum? Will you tell my mum? She won't be happy.
WILLIE	My mistake wasn't running away. It was trusting that folk would understand why I did.
HARRY	I'd like to write to Gertrude. Not seen her since I was called up in the first weeks of the war. Two years is a long time. I sometimes imagined she was here, I –
	I need to write. Say goodbye.

The CAPTAIN takes out some paper.

WILLIE   Would you take these for me? Pictures of my
                kids. And a letter. Send them to my wife. I
                wouldn't want them to get damaged.

The PRISONER'S FRIEND takes the letter and the photographs.

CAPTAIN   Is there anything else?

HARRY   No.

JOSEPH kneels on the floor.

JOSEPH   I'm sorry, Sergeant. I'm really really sorry.

SERGEANT   What the hell are you doing?

JOSEPH   I never meant it. It's all a mistake. I'm
                scared. I'm really scared. Please please
                please. I'm begging you.

JOSEPH weeps.

The SERGEANT takes a bottle from his pocket.

SERGEANT   Take this.

JOSEPH   What is it?

SERGEANT   Whisky. Got it from the missus at Christmas.
                It's not a whole lot but if you swallow it just
                before you won't know what's happening.

JOSEPH   I – I don't drink.

The SERGEANT laughs.

WILLIE   I don't believe in heroes and cowards. Not
                in war. It's only my opinion but I've been in
                it since the beginning. Because once you've
                left home, if you've never seen it, once you're
                inside it, getting smashed up in the trenches
                by the guns, you don't know who you are any
                more. Sometimes you get a medal, other times
                you get in the shit. Who decides, eh? I've seen
                blokes take on enemy trenches singlehanded.
                The day after, it's those same men who are
                broken, in tears, unable to move. Are you

telling me that's cowardice? I know the law
is the law but the law doesn't know fucking
anything about being a soldier in this place.

The SERGEANT spits, exits.

PF   Shake my hand?

WILLIE takes his hand.

CAPTAIN   B – bye, Harry.

The CAPTAIN and the PRISONER'S FRIEND exit.

JOSEPH   What – what is my mum going to say…?

25.

The firing squad march through the woods.

PRIVATE 4   **Oh my god. Where are we going?**

FIRING SQUAD   **You know, you know.**

PRIVATE 4   **Oh my god. Please don't make me go.**

FIRING SQUAD   **You know, you know.**

                     **You said it yourself, it's got to be done, a
                     man can't walk off in a battle.**

PRIVATE 4   **Oh my god. Please don't make me go. I
                     don't know if I can go through with this.**

FIRING SQUAD   **You know, you know.**

                     **What's the problem, boy? The man had
                     a trial, he's as guilty as sin. You know it's
                     not murder when you're acting under
                     orders.**

PRIVATE 4   **I don't know… Oh my god…**

FIRING SQUAD   **You know, you know.**

They arrive in the clearing in the woods.

26.

The darkest time. Before the dawn.

WILLIE writes to his sister.

WILLIE   **Dearest sister. By the time... by the time you read this, you will know... you will know the worst. I hate to bring... I hate to bring shame on you but it could not be helped. I hope one day that you will know the truth. Kiss everyone for me. Your ever loving, Willie.**

JOSEPH is drunk.

JOSEPH   **I've done a bad thing, Mum. I'm going to die, Mum.... I'm going to die Mum and I don't understand it. I said sorry. I said sorry like you taught me to. Send my love to Dad. Send my love to everyone. Your son, Joe.**

HARRY holds an envelope.

HARRY   **I've got to say goodbye Gertrude... I've got to say goodbye... I'm not afraid. I feel strong. I know who I am. I'm Harry. Your Harry. Your Harry. Always yours. I'll see you again. In a better world. Your Harry.**

He attaches the envelope to his heart. The others do the same.

The door opens. It's time.

27.

The clearing in the wood.

Before dawn.

Three six foot wooden stakes line the horizon.

The condemned men enter with their hands tied, envelopes across their hearts. HARRY, JOSEPH and WILLIE.

The FIRING SQUAD wait.

JOSEPH and WILLIE are blindfolded. HARRY refuses with a shake of his head. Each condemned man is tied to a post.

The CAPTAIN opens the bible and reads:

CAPTAIN   He was still a long way from home when his father saw him; his heart was filled with pity, and he ran, threw his arms around his son, and kissed him. Father, the son said, I have sinned against God and against you. I am no longer fit to be called your son. But the father called his servants. Hurry, he said, bring the best robe and put it on him. Put a ring on his finger and shoes on his feet. Then go and get the prize calf and kill it, and let us celebrate with a feast! For this son of mine was dead, but now he is alive; he was lost and now has been found.

The CAPTAIN closes his bible and raises his arm.

CAPTAIN   Firing Squad, attention!

The FIRING SQUAD stands to attention.

CAPTAIN   Firing Squad, present!

The FIRING SQUAD raise their rifles.

As the CAPTAIN brings his arm down, dawn breaks through the trees and light floods the clearing.

HARRY, JOSEPH and WILLIE continue until the final moment.

ALL   **I have no name
no name.**

**Cut me out,
cut me out**

like a wart
like an eye.

28.

London. The next morning. Sunny and bright. Birdsong.

GERTRUDE is making the bed when there is a knock at the door.

GERTRUDE   Coming! I won't be a moment, I –

HARRY enters, dead and covered in blood.

GERTRUDE stands absolutely still.

He moves to her and takes the envelope from his chest and holds it out.

A moment.

She reaches out to take it.

END OF PLAY

AFTERWORD: NAMING THE DEAD

There are very few things we know about the executed soldiers. Here are the facts.

Harry Farr was born in Paddington in 1891. He was one of seven brothers. He married Gertrude at Kensington Registry Office in September 1913 and their daughter, also named Gertrude, was born in December that year. Harry had already been in the Territorials for three years and was a reservist before being called up in August 1914. He saw her once again in November 1914 then never came back.

Joseph William Stones was born in 1890 in Crook and was a miner before joining up in 1915. The details of his trial are publicly available and are excellently laid out in *Blindfold and Alone* by Cathryn Corns and John Hughes-Wilson – a book I found invaluable, not only for its examination of the individual cases of the accused men but also for the context in which these executions took place. Willie (as he was to those close to him) had made a deal with a miner friend of his that if anything should happen they would look after each other's family. His friend kept his promise. Deprived of a pension after Willie's execution, his wife Isabel married Arthur Jones in December 1917.

About Joseph Byers we know even less than the others. He was born in Scotland but we do not know the date or the place. We know that he volunteered on 20th November 1914 in one of the first great patriotic waves in the early months of the war. He arrived in France on 3rd December 1914. On 8th January, Joseph went off to fetch coal and never returned. He was caught, tried for desertion and executed on 6th February 1915. He had been a soldier for fewer than three months.

Joseph's records were destroyed by bombing in the Second World War and despite the work of many historians, journalists and a genealogist employed by the National Theatre of Scotland, no family member has ever been located.

The only document that we have is Joseph's will. It's in the National Records of Scotland and I've a photocopy of it. It reads simply: 'In the event of my Death I give the whole of my stuff to my sister Nellie Murray'.

With so little documentary evidence how is it possible to write about these men?

I started by reading a lot of books about the First World War. History books, poetry, novels and letters. There was almost a hundred per cent literacy in 1914; everyone could write and they did so profusely.

There's very little testimony by the condemned men themselves. Many were too ashamed to write a letter home. Others had to ask a priest or their guard because they did not feel capable of writing that farewell missive themselves. Some were drunk on their last night. All of them were given less than 24 hours' notice of their executions. The remaining letters were hastily written goodbyes, full of sorrow and shame and apologies for what they had done.

The first-hand accounts I had at my disposal, I owe to the diligent work of my excellent researcher Sam Tranter. Sam was able to find a few eyewitness accounts of executions as well as testimonies by members of firing squads. These acts affected everyone who took part in them. They rarely spoke of it but never forgot.

What I have done in writing this play is to imagine the gaps, the spaces between the facts, and create a version of what could have been. It is not the absolute truth of what happened, nothing ever could be. But I have tried to be as honest as I know how and have based the opinions of the characters on evidence from the time. Laurie Sansom, the director, said early on in the process that I shouldn't be afraid to use the real names and stories of these people. I've often felt overawed by the responsibility to Harry, Willie and Joe but never doubted the vital importance of remembering their stories.

Oliver Emanuel, April 2016